IRAN AND THE ISLAMIC REVOLUTION

John King

Raintree

www.raintreepublishers.co.uk

Visit our website to find out more information about **Raintree** books.

To order:
 Phone 44 (0) 1865 888112
 Send a fax to 44 (0) 1865 314091
 Visit the Raintree bookshop at **www.raintreepublishers.co.uk** to browse our catalogue and order online.

Produced for Raintree by
Monkey Puzzle Media Ltd.
Gissing's Farm, Fressingfield
Suffolk IP21 5SH, UK

First published in Great Britain by Raintree,
Halley Court, Jordan Hill, Oxford OX2 8EJ,
part of Harcourt Education.
Raintree is a registered trademark of Harcourt
Education Ltd.

Edited by Jenny Siklós and Paul Mason
Designed by Tim Mayer
Picture Research by Lynda Lines and Frances Bailey
Production by Duncan Gilbert
The consultant, Dr. Robert Stern, works as a part-time
analyst for the US State Department, primarily as part
of the War on Terror. He is a former Associate
Director for Counter-Terrorism.

Originated by Modern Age
Printed and bound in China by South China
Printing Company Ltd

ISBN 1 844 43206 8
10 09 08 07 06
10 9 8 7 6 5 4 3 2 1

British Library Cataloguing in Publication Data
King, John, 1939-
Iran and the Islamic revolution. - (The Middle East)
1.Iran - History - Revolution, 1979 - Juvenile
literature 2.Iran - History - 1979-1997 - Juvenile
literature 3.Iran - History - 1997- - Juvenile
literature 4.Iran - Politics and government - 1979-
1997 - Juvenile literature 5.Iran - Politics and
government - 1997- - Juvenile literature
I.Title
955'.054

Acknowledgements
The author and publisher are grateful to the
following for permission to reproduce copyright
material: Camera Press p. **4** (Jacques Haillot);
Corbis pp. **1** (Françoise de Mulder), **7** (Hulton-
Deutsch Collection), **12** (Sygma), **14** (Christine
Spengler), **15** (Owen Franken), **17** (Christine
Spengler), **19** (Bettmann), **20** (Mohsen Shandiz/
Sygma), **22** (Roger Wood), **25** (Françoise de
Mulder), **27** (Christine Spengler), **29** (Christine
Spengler), **32** (Michel Setboun), **34** (Henry
Cleveland), **45** (Morteza Nikoubazl/Reuters), **47**
(Kaveh Kazemi); Empics pp. **8** (Nabil Mounzer/
EPA), **21** (AP), **28** (Steve Eisen/AP), **31** (PA), **37**
(Hans Edinger/AP), **40** (EPA), **43** (EPA); Getty
Images pp. **10** (Dmitri Kessel/Time & Life
Pictures), **16** (Keystone), **18** (Arnold Sachs/AFP),
42 (Mark Wilson); Reuters pp. **9** (Morteza
Nikoubazl), **38**, **39**, **46** (Morteza Nikoubazl);
Rex Features pp. **5** (SIPA), **11** (SIPA), **33** (SIPA);
Topfoto pp. **13**, **35** (Richard Ellis/The Image
Works), **36**.

Cover photograph shows spectators looking
through openings in a large banner showing
a portrait of Ayatollah Khomeini (Empics/Saleh
Rifai/AP).

Map illustrations by Encompass Graphics Ltd.

Every effort has been made to contact copyright
holders of any material reproduced in this book.
Any omissions will be rectified in subsequent
printings if notice is given to the publishers.

The paper used to print this book comes from
sustainable resources.

Contents

Some words are shown in **bold**, like this. You can find out what they mean by looking in the Glossary.

The Return of the Ayatollah

Ayatollah Khomeini returned to **Iran** to become its new leader in 1979. It was one of the most remarkable events in Iran's history. The Ayatollah's return was to change Iran completely.

On the day of his return, Ayatollah Khomeini was 76 years old. He wore plain black robes, and had a long, grey beard. For him the frenzy of the crowd was a tiring ordeal. He started his trip into the city by car, but had to be taken the last part of the way by helicopter, because there were so many people in the streets.

AYATOLLAH KHOMEINI

Ayatollah Khomeini was the most senior world leader of the **Shi'ite** branch of Islam. On 1 February 1979, he returned to Iran after a long **exile** to set up a new Islamic Republic. By the time his plane from Paris, France landed at Tehran airport, three million people were waiting to greet him. It was the largest crowd ever to gather in the Iranian capital. Around the country there was extreme excitement at the greatest political change Iran had ever seen.

❝ This is not an ordinary government. It is a government based on Islamic law. ❞
(Ayatollah Khomeini at his first press conference, on 5 February 1979)

Ayatollah Khomeini (centre of picture, with grey beard and black turban) meets his people after returning to Iran in 1979.

The return of the Ayatollah came at the end of a long period of unrest in Iran against its former ruler, the Shah. Under the Shah Iran had been a friend to the West in general, and to the USA in particular. When the Shah fled Iran in 1979, it meant the Ayatollah could return home. From the beginning of the Ayatollah's new **Islamic** Republic, the USA and Iran became enemies.

The USA was worried that Iran might create political problems in the Middle East. It was also anxious about the supply of oil. (Iran was a major oil-exporting country.) Meanwhile, Iran's new government soon began to refer to the USA as 'The Great Satan'. Iran's rulers felt that the USA interfered everywhere in the world, and tried to get what it wanted by deception and lies, if necessary. The religious leaders were particularly concerned that the attractions of American culture were tempting young people away from **Islam**.

> **❝ I have done more for Iran than any Shah for 2,000 years... you cannot compare me with these people. ❞**
> (The last Shah of Iran, Mohammed Reza Pahlavi, speaking about the new Islamic leaders before leaving Tehran on 16 January 1979)

A crowd in Tehran pulls down a statue of the Shah, Iran's last king. The Shah was hated for repressing the people and for the actions of his secret police force.

Iranian History

The history of Iran, or **Persia** as it was previously called, stretches back 2,500 years. The country was founded by the Persian King Cyrus the Great in 550 BCE. Ancient Persia was one of the great civilizations of the world.

Before the arrival of Islam, Persians followed the religion of **Zoroastrianism** (see panel). The Islamic religion began to replace Zoroastrianism in 637 CE, when a Muslim Arab army defeated the Persian defenders. The Persians remained a separate people from the Arabs, however, even though both are mainly Muslim. The Persians still speak their own language, which is different from Arabic.

After the Prophet Mohammed died in 632 CE, Islam split into two groups: **Sunnis** and Shi'ites (see page 8). Unlike its neighbouring countries, Iran followed Shi'ism. From the 16th century on, Shi'ite Islam has been the official religion of Iran. Over the centuries, Iran managed to remain independent partly because of Shi'ism, as well as the facts that it had its own language and was never invaded by the Ottoman Turks.

ZOROASTRIANISM

Zoroaster was a priest who said that men and women should worship a good spirit, Ahura Mazda, the bringer of light and life. They should turn their backs on the evil spirit, Ahriman. In Zoroastrianism human beings must choose between the good and the bad god.

Iran and its Neighbours

Iran and its neighbours. Iran borders Pakistan and Afghanistan to the east and Iraq and Turkey to the west.

> **❝** If you have any complaints about the changes I have made in this country, make them to my face. **❞**
>
> *(Reza Shah, speaking to Persian politicians in 1921)*

Reza Shah Pahlavi, the father of the last Shah of Iran and the first of the Pahlavi dynasty.

The ruler of Iran had been known since ancient times as the Shah. The Shah was an emperor or king. In 1914 the British government bought a share of the company then searching for oil in Iran, the Anglo-Persian Oil Company. During World War I (1914–1918), Great Britain and Germany – who were at war with each other – tried to influence Iran. They often ignored the Shah's authority.

In 1925 a tough military man, Colonel Reza Khan, became the first of a new and stronger **dynasty** of Shahs. Reza Shah Pahlavi, as he became known, helped Iran to regain its independence from outside powers and restore its national **sovereignty**. He strengthened the army and insisted that all people obeyed the law.

> **❝** History suggests that the Persians ... will become a strong nation. **❞**
>
> *(Ayatollah Khomeini, at his first press conference on 5 February 1979)*

Shi'ism in Iran

Iran has been a strongly religious country ever since its people became Muslims. Following the death of Mohammed, the founder of Islam, the Muslim community split in 656 CE. The majority, known today as Sunnis, supported the idea of leadership based on ability. A minority, known as the Shi'a (or 'faction'), supported a leadership based on family ties to the Prophet Mohammed.

Shi'ism was founded by Ali, the Prophet Mohammed's son-in-law and cousin. Some Muslims thought Ali was the leader of Islam. Ali was murdered in 661 CE, and is buried in the Iraqi city of Najaf. In 680 CE, his son Hussein was also killed, in the Iraqi city of Karbala. Hussein was fighting for the right to lead the Muslims. These murders started the split in Islam known as the 'Shi'a' (or 'faction'). From the 1500s on, Shi'ite Islam was the official religion of Persia.

The great mosque in Karbala, built on the site of Hussein's tomb. Both this tomb, and that of Ali, are holy places for all Shi'ites.

The annual ceremony of *Ashura*. Each year Shi'ite Muslims beat themselves with whips, weeping in memory of the death of Hussein, the Prophet Mohammed's grandson, in 680 CE.

> ❝ Like any revolutionary party, Shi'ism had ... clear principles and a strong organization. It led the deprived people in their search for freedom and justice. ❞
> *(Ali Shariati, an Iranian Islamic nationalist)*

Shi'ite and Sunni Islam agree on the basics of their religion, but over the years they have moved apart in other ways. Shi'ite Muslims have their own ways of interpreting Islamic law and Islamic custom. For example, they hold spectacular festivals, such as *Ashura*, when young men beat themselves with chains until they bleed, to show their grief at the memory of Hussein's death.

Iran is the only country where Shi'ite Islam is the official religion, and the Shi'ite faith is well organized. The ayatollahs, the most senior figures, issue judgements on legal and moral questions. The Iranian city of Qom is the centre of teaching and scholarship for Shi'ites. The story of the murders of Ali and Hussein helped form the character of Shi'ite Islam. Even today Shi'ites often see themselves as being mistreated. They feel that outside their own faith, there are enemies plotting against them, just as enemies plotted against Ali and Hussein centuries ago.

UNITY IN ISLAM
All Muslims agree on the five 'pillars' of their faith. These are:
- **prayer**
- **fasting**
- **giving alms (charity)**
- **performance of the pilgrimage to Mecca**
- **that there is only one God, and Mohammed is his Prophet.**

9

The Last Shah

In 1941 a new ruler took power in Iran. This was Mohammed Reza Shah Pahlavi, the son of Reza Shah Pahlavi, who had been forced to **abdicate** by the UK and the Soviet Union in 1941, during World War II.

After the end of World War II, the new Shah wanted to turn Iran into a more modern country. He encouraged politics, and allowed elections for **parliament**. Political parties appeared, and workers organized themselves into **trade unions**, though in 1949, the Communist Party was banned.

The Iranian oil industry developed rapidly during this period. However, there were few benefits for Iran as most of the oil profits went to the foreign-owned Anglo-Persian Oil Company. In 1951 Iran's prime minister, Mohammed Mossadegh, **nationalized** the oil industry so that Iran could control and benefit from its own oil. In 1953 Mossadegh was forced out of office with Western help, particularly from the **CIA**.

The Shah changed his approach. He accepted aid from the USA, began to strengthen his armed forces and suppressed political parties that didn't agree with his policies. From 1953 onwards, he carefully controlled Iran's government. In 1957 he set up a secret police force, known as SAVAK.

Foreign and Iranian workers shut off the oil pipes at Iran's oil centre in Abadan, before leaving the oil installation to be controlled by the Iranian government.

> **" The Shah had contempt for traditional Islam, and showed it. "**
> *(Desmond Harney, a British ex-diplomat who was in Iran in 1979)*

> **" The Shi'ite clergy are the enemies of progress. "**
> *(The Shah speaking in the 1970s)*

The last Shah leaves Iran on 16 January 1979. A soldier bends down to try to kiss the Shah's shoe.

In 1963 the Shah launched a package of **reforms** known as the 'White Revolution', which included **land reform**, **literacy** and women's rights. This led to clashes with the Muslim **clergy**, including Ayatollah Khomeini, who did not want social change in Iran. In 1964 the Ayatollah was sent into exile.

In 1971 the Shah held a huge celebration of 2,500 years of monarchy, in the ancient city of Persepolis. Many Muslims thought the celebrations were **blasphemous**, and opposition to the Shah grew. In 1975 the Shah banned political parties, but the clergy began to preach sermons against the Shah. Thousands of Iranians, including many young people, demonstrated against the government. Finally, in 1979, after strikes and riots, the Shah had to abandon his throne and flee from the country.

THE 'WHITE REVOLUTION'

The 'White Revolution' was Mohammed Reza Shah's attempt to move his country into the modern era. Land reform was popular, but other reforms that seemed pro-Western angered the clergy. The clerics did not want non-Muslim ideas to spread. For example, they opposed greater rights for women on the grounds that this would be against Islamic teachings.

11

Ayatollah Khomeini

By 1979 opposition to the Shah had been coming mainly from Islamic groups. Ayatollah Khomeini was the most important religious leader amongst these groups. What were this powerful man's origins, and when did he begin his political career?

Ayatollah Khomeini was born on 24 September 1902 in the village of Khomein in central Iran. His name at birth was Ruhollah Musavi, but he later took the name Khomeini, meaning 'from Khomein'.

Khomeini's education was religious. He studied and taught in the city of Qom, a great centre of Shi'ite Islamic teaching in Iran. Khomeini lived in a college town known as the Dar al-Shafa, and specialized in philosophy. He also married and became the father of two sons and three daughters. Soon Khomeini took his first steps in politics. In 1944 he published a book that criticized Iran's rulers, the Shahs. In the 1950s Khomeini achieved the religious rank of Ayatollah.

Khomeini as a young cleric, aged 25.

❝ I must serve Islam and the nation of Iran, and I am obliged to fulfill my divine and spiritual duty. ❞
(Khomeini in 1978, speaking in exile)

In the early 1960s, Khomeini began to oppose the rule of the Shah on the grounds that it was anti-Islamic. In 1963 he was arrested after making a fiery speech against the Shah. In 1964 the government sent him into exile in Turkey. He moved from there to the Shi'ite holy city of Najaf in Iraq, where he continued his political activities.

Khomeini had to leave Iraq in 1978, when the Shah asked the Iraqi government to halt his political activities. He was refused entry to Kuwait and flew to Paris, France on an Iraqi aircraft. He was granted temporary residence, apparently after the French authorities consulted the Shah. In France he continued to work for the Shah's downfall.

In 1963 there were riots against the Shah's attempts to introduce reforms. The Shah's plans for social change were opposed by the Shi'ite clerics.

ALLIES

Khomeini's closest political colleagues were Ayatollah Khamene'i, who became leader after his death, and Hojjatoleslam Ali Akbar Rafsanjani, later president of Iran. (Hojjatoleslam, which means 'Proof of Islam', is the rank below ayatollah). All these ranks amongst the Shi'ite clergy depend on the judgement of other clerics, who acknowledge the ability and holiness of their colleagues.

❝ We have come to the conclusion that the Shah and his regime are against Islam and the religious leadership. ❞

(Khomeini in 1978, speaking in exile)

The Islamic Revolution

The Ayatollah Khomeini returned to Iran in February 1979. An **interim** prime minister, Mehdi Bazargan, took over the running of Iran until a new government could be set up.

The interim government held a **referendum** on 30 March 1979, when the people overwhelmingly voted, in an apparently fair poll, for Iran to become an Islamic Republic. Khomeini's first task was to reorganize Iran, based on Islamic principles. This became known as the 'Islamic Revolution'.

At first, Khomeini was based in Qom. In March 1979 he set up the Revolutionary Council, mainly made up of clerics. He also established the Revolutionary Guards. At this chaotic time, violence was widespread in Iran, between individuals and even between rival revolutionary organizations. Many Iranians fled abroad, if they had the money to do so.

> ❝ **All authority aside from that which came from Khomeini was melting away.** ❞
> *(Mohammed Hassanein Heikal, a senior Egyptian journalist visiting Iran)*

Women members of the Revolutionary Guard. Both women and men supported the Islamic Revolution.

In the early years, the Islamic regime executed many opponents. These demonstrators, photographed in New York in 1982, would be thrown into prison if ever caught in Iran.

POLITICAL REPRESSION

Opposition to Iran's new rulers was stamped out ruthlessly during 1979 and 1980. Hundreds of officials of the former government were killed, and across the country hundreds, if not thousands, were executed after trials. In 1980 Khomeini began to bring this violence under control, forbidding Islamic courts to order death sentences.

Ayatollah Khomeini had thought carefully during his exile about how an Islamic state could be run. Since the days of Mohammed himself, no Muslim state had been run on Islamic principles. Many features of Iran's new constitution had to be adapted to modern circumstances, including a place for **democracy**.

A referendum in December 1979 approved Iran's new Islamic **constitution**. Ayatollah Khamene'i became Iran's new president in 1981. The country was still very unstable, with different groups competing for power. In 1981 Khomeini moved to Tehran, to strengthen his grip on the day-to-day running of the country.

> **❝ As many as a million people may have left Iran. ❞**
> (Desmond Harney, former British diplomat in Tehran)

The New Islamic Republic

The constitution of the Islamic Republic of Iran was hard to write. No previous state had ever had a government based entirely on Islam. In the end the constitution allowed people to vote, but it gave final power to the Muslim clerics.

The democratic elements of the constitution included a president who was elected by the people, and an elected parliament.

The religious elements of the constitution were designed to make sure that Iran was governed by Muslim ideas. The most important religious job was given to Khomeini himself. He became the 'supreme leader', the highest authority, not just in religious affairs, but in everything else, too. Ayatollah Khomeini set up new religious councils and committees, some partially elected, with wide-ranging powers.

> **❝ Religion gives eternal values. It does not make laws. ❞**
> *(Mohammed Mojtahed Shabestari, questioning the Islamic Constitution)*

A demonstration in 1980 shows the popular backing for Khomeini and the new Islamic Republic. Most of these demonstrators, however, would have been members of the Revolutionary Guard, making them supporters of Khomeini.

Iran emerged from its Islamic Revolution as a more democratic country than many others in the Middle East. Though Islam was the dominant power, and the supreme leader always had the final say, many issues were decided by the elected parliament. Women had to wear acceptable Islamic dress and were subjected to some restrictions, but they also had the vote, and a few women became members of parliament.

Out of the 268 seats in parliament, five are reserved for Iran's religious minorities: the Jews, the Christians and the Zoroastrians (Iran's ancient pre-Islamic faith). The **Baha'i** faith, which originated in Iran, is regarded by Islam as a **heresy** and is not recognized.

Muslim women learning to read at a revolutionary school. Under the Shah, women's literacy was low. The Islamic regime wanted all women to be able to read and write.

> **❝ Music corrupts the minds of our youth, and creates laziness. If you want the country to be independent, ban music. ❞**
> (Ayatollah Khomeini)

A NEW SYSTEM OF GOVERNMENT
- **The Iranians decided that responsibility for the country belonged to God, not to the people. The government was God's representative on Earth.**
- **The Islamic Revolution would be exported to other Muslim countries.**
- **Support for the Islamic Republic came from the clergy, the country people and the working people of Tehran.**
- **The Republic took a strong interest in the private behaviour of its citizens.**

The Islamic Republic and the Outside World

Most countries quickly accepted the Islamic Republic of Iran as an official country. Iran had previously been a major trading partner with both Europe and the USA. No one outside Iran was sure whether this situation would continue.

Before the revolution, close links had existed between the USA and the Shah. This led the Islamic revolutionaries to be hostile towards the USA. Personally Khomeini detested the USA. However, in the early months of the Islamic Republic, Iran criticized the USA very little. Iran's new government cancelled the military treaty the Shah had signed with the Americans. Despite this, US President Carter still thought the USA might be able to maintain its links with Iran.

Elsewhere Iran had a long history of trade and cultural ties with Germany. Iran also had links with France. Iran seemed to want to keep its links with Europe. For their part, the European countries were ready to work with the Islamic Republic.

US President Jimmy Carter. During his presidency, relations between the USA and Iran would become very unfriendly.

" President Carter was instinctively a peacemaker and a reformer. He rejected policies that could have resulted in US military intervention, and refused to intervene in what might have been a civil war in Iran. "
(Gary Sick, All Fall Down: America's Fateful Encounter with Iran, *1985)*

Closer to Iran, the Arab states of the Gulf of Arabia were alarmed by the revolution. Iran was a powerful and threatening state. Its aim of exporting the Islamic Revolution made it seem dangerous. Other Arab Muslim countries were also wary, especially those with Shi'ite populations. They feared that Iran would support Shi'ite attempts to start revolutions in their countries.

In the Middle East, the Iranian revolution put an end to ties between Iran and Israel, and Iran began to support the Palestinians. Iran also became involved with Lebanon, especially after Israel invaded Lebanon in 1982. Many people in southern Lebanon were Shi'ite Muslims, and Iran backed their anti-Israeli guerrilla movement known as **Hezbullah**, 'The Party of God'.

REVOLUTIONARY LINKS

The Iranian Republic quickly made links with other revolutionary movements. For example, in February 1979 the Palestinian leader Yasser Arafat was welcomed to Iran. The Islamic leadership gave the Palestinians a building that had been used by the Israelis before the revolution. The Palestinians flew the Palestinian flag from it.

ff Are we to be trampled underfoot by the boots of America, simply because we are a weak nation and have no dollars? JJ
(Ayatollah Khomeini in 1964)

An Iranian Basihi (an Islamic fighter) guards Americans at Tehran airport who are leaving Iran in February 1979.

The American Hostage Crisis

On 4 November 1979, a mob of demonstrators occupied the US Embassy in Tehran. All hope of a good relationship between Iran and the USA came to an end with the US Embassy siege.

At 10:30 in the morning, a large crowd of young Iranians swarmed into the embassy compound and into the building. The diplomatic personnel at first retreated to the upper floors of the building, then surrendered to the mob. Several senior US diplomats were at the Iranian foreign ministry at the time and remained there throughout the hostage crisis.

The group who held the embassy called themselves revolutionary students. They were protesting against the US decision to let the Shah into the USA for hospital treatment, and demanded his return to Iran to face trial. The students were also hostile to the USA, and wanted to make sure there were bad relations between their Islamic leaders and the USA.

ʺ The Americans cannot do a thing! ʺ
(Ayatollah Khomeini comments on the difficulties faced by the Americans in the hostage crisis in 1979)

American diplomatic staff being held hostage at the US Embassy in Tehran on 4 November 1979.

U.S CAN NOT DO ANYTHING

امریکا هیچ غلطی نمیتواند بکند

Jubilant Iranians show their defiance of the USA after the US Embassy had been seized and its staff taken hostage by Iranian demonstrators.

Ayatollah Khomeini did not know in advance that the US Embassy was going to be attacked. He kept quiet at first, but later gave his approval of the attack.

People in the USA were extremely angry, but there was little they could do. For the first time, the USA introduced **sanctions** against Iran in an attempt to force the release of the hostages.

In the end, the hostages were held for a total of 444 days, and a rescue attempt by US forces failed. Khomeini appeared to make the crisis into a personal fight against President Carter. He did not allow the hostages to be released until Carter's successor, President Reagan, took office.

A RESCUE MISSION THAT FAILED

On 24 April 1980, a raiding party of US helicopters took off from the US aircraft carrier *Nimitz* in the Gulf. Their mission was to rescue the hostages by force. A secret airfield had been prepared in the Iranian desert. There the helicopters were to refuel, before taking US special forces to Tehran. But a helicopter collided with a refuelling aircraft and five airmen died. The force withdrew without completing its mission.

Oil and the Islamic Revolution

In the last days of the Shah's regime, oil production had fallen to as little as 250,000 barrels a day, from its normal level of five million barrels. Strikes and disturbances had interrupted Iran's key industry. Making sure that oil would begin to flow again was one of the new government's first concerns.

Iran's Islamic leaders knew that that they needed to sell oil to pay for their plans to change the country. Oil exports from Iran began again in March 1979, three weeks after the beginning of the Revolution.

Oil tankers are loaded at the Iranian oil port of Kharg Island, on the Red Sea.

❝ The United States was importing 700,000 barrels a day from Iran... ❞
(*Gary Sick in* All Fall Down: America's Fateful Encounter with Iran, *explaining how important Iranian oil was to the USA*)

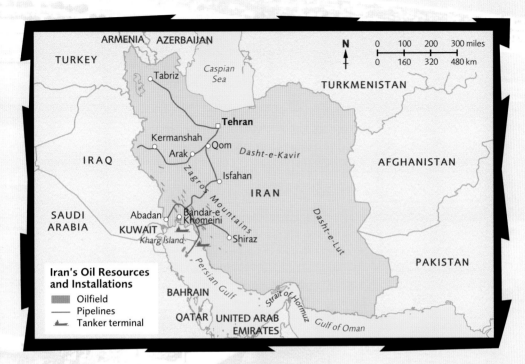

The following cities and features are labeled on the map:

ARMENIA, AZERBAIJAN, TURKEY, Tabriz, *Caspian Sea*, TURKMENISTAN, Tehran, Kermanshah, Qom, Arak, *Dasht-e-Kavir*, IRAQ, Isfahan, AFGHANISTAN, IRAN, *Zagros Mountains*, SAUDI ARABIA, Abadan, Bandar-e Khomeini, KUWAIT, *Kharg Island*, Shiraz, *Dasht-e-Lut*, PAKISTAN, BAHRAIN, *Persian Gulf*, QATAR, UNITED ARAB EMIRATES, *Strait of Hormuz*, *Gulf of Oman*

N
0 100 200 300 miles
0 160 320 480 km

Iran's Oil Resources and Installations
- Oilfield
- Pipelines
- Tanker terminal

This map shows Iran's oil installations, including pipelines. Iran's major oil deposits are in the south-west of the country.

The National Iranian Oil Company went on selling oil to its existing customers, many of them Western companies. In September 1979 the Islamic Republic set up an Oil Ministry to run its oil industry. The new government increased production to over three million barrels a day by the end of 1979. One crucial reason for the oil industry's success was that the oil workers did a good job of running the industry, even though many senior officials had fled the country.

IRAN'S OIL RESERVES
In 1979 Iran's known oil reserves were 48 billion barrels, and before the Islamic Revolution, it produced 5 million barrels per day. In 2005 Iran's known oil reserves were up to 130 billion barrels. It produces 3.8 million barrels per day, which means it can continue to pump oil for 93 years at the present level. Iran also produces natural gas.

❝ Iran is globally considered as one of the world's major oil producers and exporters. ❞
(Iranian Oil Ministry)

War Between Iran and Iraq

The Islamic Republic soon found itself entangled in a war against a neighbouring country, Iraq. The war began in September 1980, when Iraqi troops invaded south-west Iran. The result was a conflict that sapped Iran's resources.

Iran was not the only country in which the regime had changed in 1979. In Iraq, Iran's western neighbour, Saddam Hussein took over as president. His actions as a **dictator** would come to have a major impact on the region and the world.

In 1979 Iraq had a number of long-standing arguments with Iran. First, Iraq demanded increased use of the Shatt el-Arab waterway, which marks the southernmost stretch of the frontier between the two countries. Second, Iraq made a territorial claim to Khuzestan, the oil-rich Iranian province bordering on Iraq. Some of Khuzestan's people were Arabic-speaking, and Iraq thought that they should be part of Iraq, not Iran. Third, Saddam Hussein feared that Iran might encourage rebellion amongst Iraq's own Shi'ite population, which made up more than half of Iraq's people.

This map shows territorial gains made by both sides in the region of the Shatt el-Arab waterway during the Iran-Iraq War. The shading shows the greatest extent of the territory that was captured by each side.

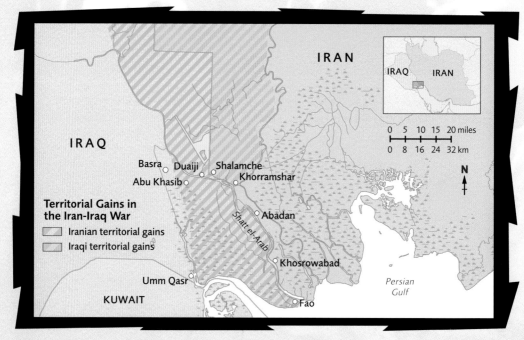

IRAN

IRAQ   IRAN

0 5 10 15 20 miles
0 8 16 24 32 km

N

IRAQ

Basra   Duaiji   Shalamche
Abu Khasib   Khorramshar

Territorial Gains in the Iran-Iraq War
- Iranian territorial gains
- Iraqi territorial gains

Shatt el-Arab

Abadan

Khosrowabad

Umm Qasr

KUWAIT   Fao

Persian Gulf

> **❝** Some Iranian volunteers even carried their own burial shrouds to the front in the expectation of martyrdom, and all fought bravely. **❞**
> *(Propaganda from the Iran Information Centre.*
> *In Shi'ite Islam, dying a martyr is seen as noble.)*

Saddam Hussein thought that Iran would be weak immediately after the Islamic Revolution. He also thought that Iran's armed forces, built up by the Shah, and equipped and trained by the USA, might be unwilling to fight for Ayatollah Khomeini. On 22 September 1980 he attacked Iran. But Iran fought back, soon seizing territory inside Iraq.

Iranian volunteers at the front showing their defiance of the Iraqis. Up to half a million young Iranians died in the conflict.

Iraq quickly got into difficulties. Iraq's army was professional, highly trained and well equipped. Iran, however, was able to organize a vast people's army to fight off the Iraqi attack. Iran's Shi'ite culture, where **martyrs** were honoured, meant that Iranians were willing to go to the front to fight and die. In addition Iran's religious leadership hated the Iraqi regime, which it saw as an enemy of Islam.

THE WEST AND THE WAR
In the Iran-Iraq war, the Western world said it was **neutral**, but in reality, backed Iraq. The hostage crisis (see pages 20–21) had made Iran seem a real danger to the West. More importantly the USA feared that Iran could make a grab for territory and oil resources in the Gulf, where there were large Shi'ite Muslim populations in the oil states.

The End of the Iran-Iraq War

War raged back and forth between Iran and Iraq for eight years. The fighting against Iraq, an outside enemy, helped Iranians unite under the new Islamic Republic.

The war was long and hard. After an Iranian attack on the key Iraqi city of Basra, the Iraqis fought back, driving the Iranians back out of Iraqi territory. The two sides fired long-range missiles at each other's cities and sank each other's ships. By 1988 neither side had made any big gains.

The overall cost of the war was huge. There are no definite figures, but estimates of the total number of dead on both sides range from 500,000 up to a million. More than half the dead were Iranians. The cost to the economies of the two sides was also terrible. Oil production was badly hit in both countries. In Iran it fell to around two million barrels a day, and much of this was needed at home for the war effort. This left Iran unable to sell oil abroad, and so the country was very short of money.

In 1988 Saddam Hussein, with his country exhausted by war, asked for an end to the fighting. A truce was declared and negotiators for the two sides met to agree a peace in the Swiss city of Geneva on 25 August 1988.

After Iraq's invasion of nearby Kuwait in 1990, Iraq no longer wanted to be on bad terms with its other neighbours. Iran agreed to restore diplomatic relations and good terms. The situation was returned to how it had been before the war began.

During the Iran-Iraq war, relations between Iran and the West had become even worse. The USA and Europe had declared themselves to be neutral, but had in fact helped Iraq. Iran's hostility towards the USA deepened still further.

THE *VINCENNES* INCIDENT

One particular reason for bad feeling between Iran and the USA was an incident in the Gulf on 3 July 1988 involving the US warship *Vincennes*. A civilian Iranian passenger plane flying from Bandar Abbas in Iran to Dubai was mistaken for a hostile Iranian jet fighter, and was shot down, killing 290 people.

Families of those who died in the Iran-Iraq war visit the martyrs' cemetery. Many women lost husbands, brothers and sons.

"Today the Iranian nation understands that the enemy has been defeated because it has failed to weaken Iran after eight years of war."
(Iran's President Khamene'i, August 1988)

Human Rights In Iran

From the outset, the Islamic Republic of Iran was criticized in the West for its attitude to human rights. The Republic's Islamic courts, and their death sentences on those who opposed the revolution, were notorious.

Human rights, as defined by the **United Nations**, include the right to liberty under the law, equality and freedom of movement. A person has a right to a fair and open trial, and to be free from the threat of torture. Other protected rights are the freedom to hold one's own opinions, to speak and write and to meet in groups to talk and act together.

Western concern over threats to human rights in Iran has continued for many reasons. Although Khomeini ended the extreme strictness of the Islamic courts in 1980, judgements and sentences in the justice system still seemed too harsh to Western eyes. The religious police, called the *mutaww'in* in **Persian**, placed many controls on people's lives, telling them how to dress and how to behave in public, for example. The Islamic Republic reacted violently to political opposition. Iranian opponents of the Republic were hunted down and some were killed, even those who were living abroad.

The Islamic Revolution hunted down Iranians abroad who were opposed to Iran's new government. Here the body of an Iranian militant murdered at his home in the state of Maryland, USA, is removed by police and paramedics.

❝ The purpose of Islam is not enjoyment. ❞
(Ayatollah Khomeini)

Iran's government also controlled the country's cultural life. The arts and entertainment were very limited. Music was not forbidden in the Islamic Republic, but Western pop music was banned. The subjects of films were restricted, though Iranian films continued to be popular. Iranian writers still have to be very careful about what they put in their books.

Women's rights were restricted after the Revolution, though they were allowed to take part in politics. Controls were put on women's behaviour: they had to cover themselves up completely with a black robe, known in Persian as a *chador*, when outside their homes. Meanwhile, though women were encouraged to go to school and allowed to go on to college, only 10 per cent of women went on to work outside the home.

Iranian women at the polling booths prepare to vote. The Islamic regime has a strong element of democracy, though the ruling clerics keep control.

❝ We deserve to join the rest of the world. We deserve opportunities like everyone else. ❞
(An anonymous opponent of the Iranian regime speaking on an Internet site)

WOMEN IN IRAN TODAY

Before 1979 only 55 per cent of women in Iran's towns could read, and only 10 per cent in the countryside. By 2005, 97 per cent of the population could read, including women. Women's life expectancy was 72 in 2005, ten years more than in 1979.

The Rushdie Affair

In February 1989 a sudden development caused even greater problems between Iran and the West. Ayatollah Khomeini pronounced a **fatwa** against the writer Salman Rushdie. The fatwa said it was legal to kill Rushdie, who the Ayatollah felt to have committed blasphemy in one of his books.

Rushdie's book, *The Satanic Verses*, had been published in London in September 1988. The author was a British writer whose family were Muslims from India. In the following months, the Muslim community in the UK, and then around the world, greeted the book with outrage. It was burned in the streets of Bradford, where many Muslims live.

Many Muslims believed that *The Satanic Verses* was disrespectful towards the Prophet Mohammed and the **Qur'an**. Muslims believe that the Muslim holy book, the Qur'an, was given to Mohammed by the Angel Gabriel. *The Satanic Verses* hinted that some of the verses of the Qur'an might not be real revelations from God. The book suggests that sometimes the Devil may have disguised himself to give Mohammed false ideas. This idea is deeply offensive to Muslims. Khomeini issued his fatwa on 14 February 1989.

Salman Rushdie went into hiding immediately. Shortly after this an organization in Iran offered a reward of US$3 million to anyone who killed him. The British government and other European states reacted with outrage. Iran withdrew its ambassadors from the countries of the **European Union** in March 1989, while the UK broke off diplomatic relations for more than a year.

Salman Rushdie was given police protection in the UK, and for several years lived in hiding. As time has passed, the immediate threat that anyone might attempt to carry out the fatwa has lessened, and his life has become less restricted. He still keeps his whereabouts secret, however. The Rushdie affair meant that there were very bad relations for a while between several European countries and Iran.

WHAT A FATWA MEANS

A fatwa is an opinion on a religious question, issued by an Islamic authority recognized by Muslim scholars. It can relate to any kind of issue where a religious opinion is important. The issues may range from very important to very minor. A fatwa is only very rarely a death sentence.

The text of the fatwa:
❝ The author of *The Satanic Verses* [is] ... condemned to death. I call on all valiant Muslims wherever they may be in the world to execute this sentence without delay. ❞
(Ayatollah Khomeini)

Muslim protestors in the UK show their anger towards the writer Salman Rushdie and his book *The Satanic Verses*.

The Death of Khomeini

On 3 June 1989 Ayatollah Khomeini died. Khomeini's funeral was even more remarkable than his return from exile had been. Twelve million people filled the streets of Tehran. Some beat themselves with chains, others ran weeping all the way to the cemetery. A few even threw themselves into Khomeini's grave.

The despair of the population arose from the loss of a powerful and respected leader, who seemed impossible to replace. In fact, after ten years of the Islamic Revolution, Iran's new system was strong enough to survive the death of its creator. Many Iranians continued to support the Islamic Republic with great enthusiasm.

Khomeini had put a system in place to choose his successor. The next supreme leader was Ayatollah Khamene'i, already Iran's president. Khamene'i was a close friend of Khomeini from the early days of the Revolution. He was chosen by the Assembly of Experts, a group of senior clergy. Hojjatoleslam Rafsanjani, the former speaker of the parliament, was then elected president. Rafsanjani was president until 1997.

ff This has been a very difficult path to tread... Let me sleep. JJ
(Khomeini's last words)

The funeral of the Ayatollah Khomeini in Qom. Anyone who could get near the coffin tried to touch it, before the Ayatollah finally left them.

The state I was in that night was the hardest to endure of my whole life. Those who were gathered there, the doctors, staff, relatives, and the clergy, were sobbing their hearts out.
(Ali Akbar Rafsanjani, later president of Iran, who was present at Khomeini's death)

Ali Akbar Rafsanjani, who became president of Iran after Khomeini's death.

The Islamic Republic had shown that it could manage a peaceful handover of power. But there were changes in the post-Khomeini era. The president had more power than before, while Khamene'i, as supreme leader, stayed more in the background.

President Rafsanjani was a dedicated supporter of the Islamic Republic. Even so, he seemed likely to relax some of the Republic's strictest rules. Rafsanjani thought that Iran needed to get along better with other countries in the world, even if they did not share its views on religious issues. In the end Rafsanjani made fewer changes within Iran than had been expected, but he did try to improve Iran's relations with its neighbours.

THE SHIFT OF POWER

Supreme leader Ayatollah Khamene'i was far below Ayatollah Khomeini in the religious hierarchy, and this prevented him from having the same amount of power. Meanwhile the new president, Rafsanjani, was a clever politician who had also known Khomeini before the Islamic Revolution. This added to his power and influence.

Iran and the USA

Relations between Iran and the USA had been strained since the hostage crisis of 1979 (see pages 20–21). The situation between the two countries worsened during the Iran-Iraq war, when the USA favoured Iraq. In 1987 the confrontation reached a new crisis.

Iran and the USA clashed in the Persian Gulf, when the US Navy tried to protect neutral shipping from Iranian forces. In October 1987 the USA stepped up its sanctions on Iran. President Reagan stopped almost all imports from Iran into the USA.

The USA said Iran had refused to obey UN **Security Council** resolution 958 calling for an end to the Iran-Iraq war. The USA also accused Iran of being responsible for international terrorism. The policy of tough sanctions begun by President Reagan was continued in the 1990s by President Clinton.

There were several reasons for the clash between the USA and Iran. First was the Iranian government's attitude to human rights. The USA continued to criticize the justice system in Iran, and the ruthless actions taken against opponents of the regime.

> **❝ We have been battling against American imperialism. ❞**
> (President Rafsanjani, 1995)

A US landing craft stands alongside an Iranian ship in the Gulf in 1987. During the Iran-Iraq War Iranian vessels attacked not only Iraqi ships but also those belonging to Kuwait and other neutral countries. The USA patrolled the Gulf to maintain 'freedom of navigation'.

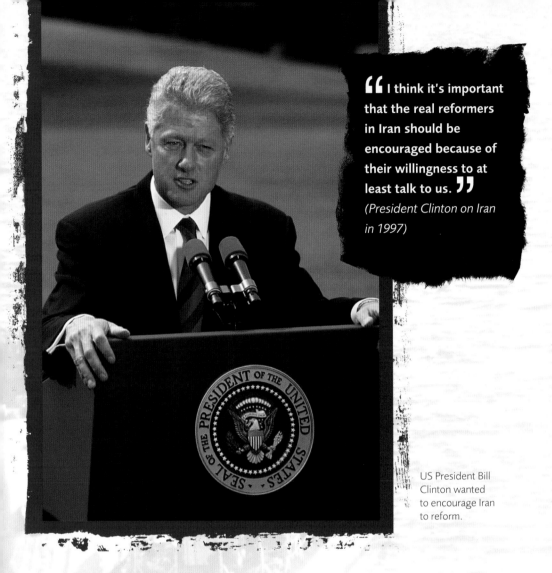

" I think it's important that the real reformers in Iran should be encouraged because of their willingness to at least talk to us. "
(President Clinton on Iran in 1997)

US President Bill Clinton wanted to encourage Iran to reform.

The USA also criticized Iran over its actions in the conflict between Israel and the Palestinians. Iran encouraged attacks on Israel by Hezbullah forces in Lebanon. The Iranians also aided radical **Islamist** resistance groups, such as Hamas and **Islamic Jihad**. The USA accused Iran of supporting violence and terrorism.

Finally, the USA saw Iran as a threat to its oil supplies from the Gulf, where Iran was building up its naval forces. Furthermore, the USA believed that Iran planned to develop **weapons of mass destruction**, or **WMD**.

In 1997, when President Khatami was elected (see pages 38–39), the US government's attitude changed slightly. President Clinton hoped that the USA and Iran could have a better relationship, providing that there were real signs of reform in Iran.

Iran and Europe

Iran had long-standing relations with many European countries, dating from the days of the Shah and before. The countries of the European Union shared US concerns about Iran. However, the Europeans decided to try bringing about change through different methods.

The Chancellor of Germany, Helmut Kohl, tried to develop what he called a 'critical dialogue' with Iran. The plan was to keep links with Iran, but to explain to the regime what the West found unsatisfactory.

European governments understood that there were problems between Iran and the USA. They knew that the hostage crisis and the confrontation between Iran and the USA in the Gulf created great difficulties between the countries. However, most European countries felt that these issues did not directly concern them.

The European Union did not follow the USA in applying sanctions on Iran. Germany in particular was eager to keep up its links with Iran. The UK and France also backed this policy. The European leaders knew that there were **moderate** groups in Iran who were struggling for power. Some of these moderates were arguing for a different, less aggressive approach in internal affairs and relations with the outside world.

> **❝ My impression is that they seem to be willing to actually have contacts and talks with the West. ❞**
>
> (Chancellor Helmut Kohl of Germany, 1991)

Iranians demonstrate in front of a court in Berlin in 1997, where a judge found that the Iranian government was involved in the killing of exiles in Berlin in 1992.

Instead of using sanctions, European leaders decided to work with the Iranian leaders, especially the moderates. Their aim was to help and encourage the moderates, and to change Iran from within.

When a new Iranian president came to power in 1997 (see pages 38–39), the European states believed that they might have an opportunity to build more useful relations with Iran. There was soon a setback, however. In 1997 a court in Berlin, Germany decided that senior Iranian government officials had been responsible for a terrorist incident in Berlin in 1992. During this incident, four members of an Iranian Kurdish opposition movement had been gunned down by assassins.

> **❝ The Islamic regime must understand that we in Europe take the human rights issue very seriously. But at the same time, we will reconsider our policy towards Iran. ❞**
>
> (Niels Petersen, Danish foreign minister)

A Time of Reform

In 1997 Rafsanjani stepped down and a new president was elected. This was Hojjatoleslam Mohammed Khatami. Born in 1943 Khatami was a leading figure in a group of younger clerics. Together they started to consider making changes to the Islamic Republic.

Elected by a huge majority (69 per cent of the votes cast), Khatami promised from the start to make real changes in Iran. He won the election thanks to the support of women and young people, and offered to improve the position of both.

Of course Khatami was a member of the clergy too. His reforms were never likely to be radical by Western standards. Nevertheless he was aware of the outside world in a way that the senior clerics had not been. He had been head of the Islamic Centre in the German city of Hamburg, and spoke both English and German, as well as Persian.

The traditional Islamic parties said that Khatami gave the press and book publishers too much freedom. He became a target for **conservatives** who aimed to preserve the Islamic Republic exactly as Khomeini had constructed it.

Conservative Iranians march to demonstrate against reform in Iran.

> **Today, the old civilization cannot be preserved. There must be change for modern times, appropriate to the circumstances.**
> *(President Khatami at the Islamic summit in Tehran, 1997)*

Iranian women support Mohammed Khatami as a candidate for president in 1997. Khatami wanted to reform Iran and allow people a freer life. He won 69 per cent of the votes.

By the late 1990s, two-thirds of Iran's population of 60 million were under the age of 30. Many of these young people hoped for change. For example women, especially in the cities, hoped for some of the same freedoms as women had in the West, such as being able to dress however they liked.

In the end, though, reform was blocked by older and more conservative clerics. Ayatollah Khomeini had created several Islamic organizations that were supposed to make sure the Islamic Republic did not stray too far from its Islamic beginnings. One of these organizations was the Council of Guardians. The Council had the power to veto (stop) proposed laws, and was full of older, conservative clerics. The conservatives were able to stop many of the changes Khatami had hoped to introduce.

POLITICAL FACTIONS IN IRAN

There are two main groups:
*   **the Islamic Left (who want social change). The main organization within this group is the Majma-e Ruhaniyun-e Mobarez, or MRM (Grouping of Militant Clerics).**
*   **the traditional Right (who are against political parties and believe the supreme leader should make all decisions). The main conservative group is the Jame-e Ruhaniyat-e Mobarez, the JRM (Society of Militant Clergy).**

Khatami's Second Term

In June 2001 President Khatami won a second election. This time he won by an even wider margin than in 1997, with 78 per cent of the votes. Change was in the air. But many conservative religious leaders, including the supreme leader himself, Ayatollah Khamene'i, opposed the reforms Khatami wanted to make.

President Khatami was re-elected in 2001. Here he casts his own vote at a polling station in Tehran.

> **The people of Iran now expect the government to take more determined steps to give them the reforms they want.**
>
> (President Khatami, after the 2001 election)

What Khatami and his supporters wanted was greater freedom of speech, less interference by the government in people's lives and more openness to the West. This sounds like a big change, but in fact all of Iran's political parties had their beginnings in the circle around the late Ayatollah Khomeini. President Khatami, though a reformer, had also been part of Khomeini's group. None of Iran's leaders wanted to make basic changes to the Islamic Republic.

FORCES AGAINST REFORM

The various conservative groups in Iran remained determined to block President Khatami's reforms. The Revolutionary Guards, the so-called *Pasdaran*, dated back to the early days of the Islamic Revolution and were a military force controlled by the supreme leader. The *Basij* was a less organized militia. There were also many young men ready to help the religious police make sure people behaved as they were meant to.

Even though differences between the ruling groups were not wide, they were still strongly felt. Iran's supreme leader, Ayatollah Khamene'i, did all he could to spoil Khatami's plans. After the parliamentary elections in 2000, he banned many newspapers. These were the ones that had been allowed by President Khatami to be critical of developments in Iran.

> **The conservatives will do battle with the reformists on all issues which they believe will endanger their interests.**
>
> (Nasser Hadian, Iranian political observer)

At the same time, the Revolutionary Guards, a military force controlled by Khamene'i, threatened to take violent action against reformists. Some young Khatami supporters were beaten up by conservative **vigilantes**, the *Basij*. In the face of constant obstruction by Khamene'i, the reform movement decided to slow down the pace of change in Iran.

Khatami had to be very careful, because of the ways in which Khamene'i could ruin his efforts (see pages 38–39). Reform still happened in Iran, but Khamene'i had given a very strong signal that he was not prepared to allow too many changes to take place.

The 'Axis of Evil'

On 11 September 2001, two hijacked passenger planes piloted by **extremist** Muslim terrorists flew into and destroyed the World Trade Center buildings in New York City. Another aircraft flew into the **Pentagon** building, and a fourth crashed in Pennsylvania before reaching its target.

The attitude of the USA to the Middle East changed dramatically after the 11 September attacks. The organizer of the attack on the World Trade Center was the **fundamentalist** Islamic terrorist leader, Osama bin Laden. The USA soon attacked bin Laden's base in Afghanistan.

The US government believed other forces in the Middle East and elsewhere in the world were hostile towards the USA. These would be targeted in what President George W. Bush called the 'War on Terror'.

❝ States like these, and their terrorist allies, constitute an Axis of Evil, arming to threaten the peace of the world. ❞
(President George W. Bush, State of the Union address, 2002)

President George W. Bush giving his State of the Union address in January 2002, when he said Iran was part of the 'Axis of Evil'.

Iran has been developing long-range missiles. This missile is the Shahab 3, which has a range of 1,400 kilometres (870 miles).

In his State of the Union speech in January 2002, the President said that three states made up what he called an 'Axis of Evil'. These were Iraq, North Korea and Iran. Iraq was an old enemy of the USA from the Gulf War, and North Korea was about to produce its first nuclear weapons.

Iran and the USA, meanwhile, had been in conflict since 1979. The President appeared to focus on the threat from Iran's nuclear programme and the possibility of it producing nuclear bombs. He also talked about allegations that Iran was allied to terrorists. Would the USA now take action against Iran? The question hung in the air, and after a US-led **coalition** invaded Iraq in March 2003, it seemed possible that an attack on Iran could follow.

A HARD LINE ON IRAN

With his State of the Union speech, President Bush seemed to raise the level of US hostility towards Iran to new heights. Previous presidents had spoken of Iran's faults, and on its need to correct them. Now Iran, in the eyes of the USA, was considered not just hostile, but evil.

Iran and Nuclear Weapons

Iran has been developing nuclear technology since before the Islamic Revolution. This has become a major reason for conflict between Iran and the USA. Since the Revolution, Iran has tried to go on with its nuclear plans, leading to fears that it could be developing nuclear weapons.

Iran's first research reactor was actually bought from the USA in 1959. The Shah planned to develop nuclear power to supply the country's energy, instead of using its oil. This would have left more oil free to sell abroad, and given Iran money for imports and development. In 1970 Iran joined the global treaty banning nuclear weapons, the Nuclear Non-Proliferation Treaty.

In 1974 Iran made a deal with Germany to build a nuclear power station at Bushehr, but after the Islamic Revolution in 1979, Germany withdrew. China helped until 1997, then Iran began to buy nuclear equipment from Russia. Despite all of this, the International Atomic Energy Agency (IAEA) has so far found no evidence of bomb building in Iran.

> **❝ It is our judgement that Iran is developing a nuclear weapon. ❞**
> (Former US Secretary of State Colin Powell, July 2004)

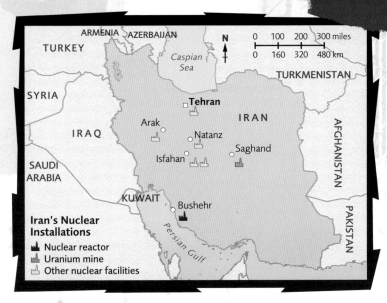

Iran's nuclear installations, showing reactors and research centres, as well as Iran's centre for uranium refinement.

Iran's Bushehr nuclear reactor under construction. The reactor is part of what Iran says is its peaceful nuclear programme that is supposed to boost Iran's electricity supply.

> **❝ As we have often said, we are not making nuclear weapons. ❞**
> *(Ayatollah Khamene'i, November 2004)*

Iran plans to make its own nuclear fuel from natural uranium. This is causing international concern. Iran wants to refine uranium to a very high level, which means it could also be used in nuclear weapons. Some reports have suggested that Iran could be close to making nuclear bombs. But Iran insists that it has no nuclear weapons programme, and has said it will allow inspections by the IAEA to prove this.

None of the Arab states has any ability to make nuclear bombs. Of the various Muslim countries, only Pakistan has nuclear weapons. The USA believes that Pakistan has supplied Iran with some nuclear technology that could be used for military purposes.

European countries have offered to supply nuclear fuel to Iran if it halts its own production programme. This would mean Iran no longer had the option of making weapons-grade fuel.

THE INTERNATIONAL ATOMIC ENERGY AGENCY

The IAEA was set up in 1957, as part of the United Nations. Its aim is to develop safe and peaceful nuclear technology. Its headquarters are in Vienna. It has a 35-member board of governors taken from the UN member states, and includes 13 states with special nuclear expertise.

Iran Faces the Future

Many uncertainties lie ahead for Iran. Its population has now grown to over 66 million. What does the future hold for these people?

Iran's constitution seems strange by Western standards, but it allows much scope for democracy and, therefore, for non-violent change. What gets in the way of this is the role of the supreme leader. The supreme leader can cancel democratic decisions. The reformers in Iran have said that their long-term aim is to enable democratically elected parties to take control. This would mean that change could not be blocked by one man.

> **❝ There are restrictions here because of religion. That slows down the pace of change, but it doesn't stop it. I believe that everyone, man or woman, should have belief in their capabilities. ❞**
> (Laleh Siddigh, a female racing driver with an engineering PhD, quoted in the British newspaper, The Guardian, 8 April 2005)

Just how contented are the people of Iran? The population is young: by 2004, 70 per cent were under the age of 30. Many of these young people hope for change. Student demonstrations in 2003 only ended after 4,000 arrests. However, after the elections of 2004 and 2005 (see feature panel), the reformers became even more isolated, making change less likely.

It is not certain whether Iran is trying to make nuclear weapons, but the technology it is developing does seem to suggest that it might be, whatever the government says.

Demonstrating students in Iran in 2004 demand that President Khatami speed up the pace of change.

> **"** Either the Islamic Revolution must mellow and embrace political change, or face a reckoning down the road when hard-line clerics come into conflict with the secular [non-religious], democratic ideals of the younger generation. **"**
> (*Afshin Molavi*, The Smithsonian, *March 2005*)

Many women in Iran work. Here young women are working in a fast-food restaurant in Tehran.

ELECTIONS IN 2004 AND 2005

Candidates for parliamentary elections must be approved by the Council of Guardians, a group dominated by conservatives. Half the members of the Council are nominated by the supreme leader. In 2004, the Council did not allow many reformers to stand in Iran's elections. This resulted in a very conservative parliament. In June 2005, things got even worse for the reformers, as the conservative Mahmoud Ahmadinejad was elected as Iran's new president.

In his 'Axis of Evil' speech (see pages 42–43), President Bush referred to Iran's links with terror organizations. But how likely is it that Iran is supporting Sunni Muslim groups such as Al-Qaeda, Osama bin Laden's terror group? There is deep distrust and even sometimes hatred between Shi'ite Muslims and Sunnis. For this reason it seems unlikely that Iran would support a Sunni organization such as Al-Qaeda.

Developments in Iran and the attitude of the USA will be crucial to the future. A particular problem is the mounting concern in the USA over Iran's nuclear plans. This may bring the two countries into conflict at some point.

One hope for the future is that Iran may be able to build better relations with European and other countries. This would make it less isolated in the international community.

Glossary

abdicate to step down from the position of king or other ruler

Baha'i religious movement originating in Iran in the nineteenth century that emphasizes the spiritual unity of mankind. It is not recognized by the government in Iran, which considers it to be heresy.

blasphemous to do something against religion, in an insulting way

CIA (Central Intelligence Agency) agency whose duty it is to inform the US government of developments abroad, and to act in the US interest

cleric, clergy men of religion

coalition group of nations or other bodies that acts together to do something

conservative describes a person who wants to avoid change in politics

constitution basic rules for how a country is governed, gathered into a single document

democracy a government in which supreme power is given to the people through a system of representation, usually involving free elections

dictator individual ruler who has complete control over a country's government and often rules harshly and violently

dynasty family of rulers, who pass power down from father to son

European Union (EU) a union of 25 independent states based on the European Community and founded to enhance political, economic and social cooperation. It was formerly known as the European Community (EC) or European Economic Community (EEC).

exile living in a foreign country after being forced to leave your own

extremist describes an individual or political group associated with opinions and practices that most people consider unacceptable. Extremists believe in forceful actions to keep or change a political situation.

fatwa Muslim declaration equivalent to law, often used to punish someone who has done something against Islam. It is rarely a death sentence.

fundamentalist describes an individual or group that believes in living strictly by a basic set of principles in a religion or belief system

heresy religious opinion that goes against the official belief of a religious authority or leader

Hezbullah means in Arabic 'Party of God'. Hezbullah is an Islamic movement started in Lebanon in the early 1980s to drive Israeli troops from Lebanon.

interim describes the period between points of time or events. An interim leader or government is put into place while a more permanent situation is being prepared for.

Iran since 1935, the country that was formerly called Persia has been known as Iran. Iran was also a name for the country in pre-classical times (before 400 BCE, when it became Persia).

Islam religion started by the Prophet Mohammed in which there is one God, Allah, and the holy book is the Qur'an. It is the main religion of the Middle East, and its followers are called Muslims.

Islamic connected with Islam

Islamic Jihad Islamic fundamentalist Palestinian resistance group set up in 1979. *Jihad* is an Arabic word that literally means struggle. It is often translated as 'holy war', in other words, a violent struggle undertaken for religious reasons.

Islamist making political use of Islam. Referring to Islam as the justification for political action or social change.

land reform when land is taken from landowners and given to the farmers who work on it

literacy being able to read and write

martyr person who voluntarily suffers death for their religion. Martyrs are greatly respected in parts of the Muslim world.

militant someone who fights for his or her beliefs

militia armed force independent of any nation or national army

moderate someone who does not have extreme opinions, in one direction or another, on political issues

nationalize when a government takes over control of an industry or business that was previously privately owned

neutral not taking sides in an argument or disagreement

parliament body of government, often made up of elected members, that comes together to create the laws of a country

Pentagon large five-sided building in Virginia, near Washington, D.C. that is the headquarters of the US Department of Defense, including all three military services: the Army, Navy and Air Force

Persia former name of Iran from classical times until 1935, when the new name was taken

Persian the language of Iran (Farsi is the Persian word). It is an Indo-European language, distantly related to the languages of Europe and North India.

Qur'an holy book of Islam, composed of sacred writings accepted by Muslims as revelations (truths) made to Mohammed by Allah (God) through the Angel Gabriel

referendum popular vote on a specific issue

reform political change, intended to improve the situation in a country

sanctions economic or military action taken by one or several nations against a nation that is breaking international law. The sanctions are intended to force the offending country to stop breaking the law.

Security Council United Nations body that takes action in a crisis to maintain peace. The Security Council consists of fifteen nations, of which five are permanent members: the USA, the UK, France, Russia and China.

Shi'ites descendants of the Muslims who accepted Ali, the prophet's son-in-law and cousin, as their leader in 656 CE. Over the centuries, they have come to have different ideas from Sunni Muslims, but agree on the basics of Islam.

sovereignty right of a government to control its own country

Sunnis followers of the mainstream Muslim faith, which rejected Ali's claim to be the leader of the Muslim world. Over the centuries, Sunnis and Shi'ites developed different customs, but they agree on all the basics of Islam.

trade unions organization of those in a trade or industry created to gain improvements in pay, benefits and working conditions

United Nations (UN) international body created in 1945, after World War II, to safeguard world peace

vigilante person who, though not a police officer, seeks to enforce the law

weapons of mass destruction (WMD) normally means nuclear, chemical and biological weapons, designed to kill as many people as possible at once. Chemical weapons are usually poisons, and biological weapons are based on germs and viruses.

Zoroastrianism Iran's ancient pre-Islamic faith. Zoroaster, a priest who lived around 600 BCE, said that men and women should worship a good spirit, Ahura Mazda, the bringer of light and life. They should turn their backs on the evil spirit Ahriman. People who follow Zoroastrianism must choose between the good and the bad god.

Facts and Figures

IRAN

GEOGRAPHY

Location: Between Iraq and Pakistan, with sea coasts on the Gulf, the Gulf of Oman (Indian Ocean) and the Caspian Sea

Area: 1,648,000 square kilometres (636,000 square miles). This is slightly larger than Alaska, just under half the total area of the 25-country European Union.

Land borders: Afghanistan, Armenia, Azerbaijan, Iraq, Pakistan, Turkey, Turkmenistan

Climate: Arid and semi-arid; subtropical in the area on the Caspian Sea coastline

Land use:

Arable and cultivated	10.1%
Uncultivated	89.9%

The land is rugged and mountainous, with deserts in the central area and small areas of plain on the coastlines.

POPULATION

Population size: 68,017,860

Age structure:

0–14 years	27.1%
15–64 years	68.0%
65 years and over	4.9%

Median age: 24.2 years

Population growth rate: 0.86%

Life expectancy at birth:

Total population	69.96 years
Male	68.58 years
Female	71.4 years

Ethnic groups:

Persian	51%
Azeri	24%
Gilaki and Mazandarani	8%
Kurd	7%
Arab	3%
Others	7%

Religions:

Muslim	98%
(consisting of Shi'ite	89%
and Sunni	9%)
Zoroastrian, Jewish, Christian and Baha'i	2%

Literacy rate (age 15 and over):

Total population	79.4%
Male	85.6%
Female	73%

ECONOMY

Most economic activity in Iran is controlled by the state. The economy is dependent on oil, and relatively high oil prices have enabled Iran to amass US$30 billion in foreign exchange reserves. However, this has had little effect on reducing unemployment or inflation. Private sector activities are generally small-scale, mainly workshops, farming and services.

GDP: US$576.7 billion

GDP growth rate: 6.3%

GDP per capita (at purchasing power parity): US$7700

This figure means that the GDP per capita in Iran in local currency would buy the same quantity of goods as would US$7700 spent in the USA.

GDP by sector:

Agriculture	11.2%
Industry	40.9%
Services	48.7%

Oil production: 3.962 million barrels per day

Oil reserves: 130.8 billion barrels

Inflation rate: 15.5%

Labour force: 23 million

The unemployment rate is 11.2% and there is a shortage of skilled labour.

(*Source:* CIA World Factbook, 2005)

Timeline

600 BCE–1980 CE

550 BCE Cyrus the Great establishes the Persian Empire in the ancient land of Iran

334 BCE Alexander the Great invades Persia

570 CE The Prophet Mohammed is born

637 CE The Persian Empire is swiftly conquered by Muslim Arab tribesmen

661 CE Ali, the Prophet Mohammed's son-in-law, is assassinated

820–1220 CE Local Persian rulers come to power. Persia becomes a key Islamic country.

1258 The Mongols sack Baghdad

1501–1524 Shah Ismail I takes control of Persia. Shi'ism becomes the state religion.

1851–1906 The Qajars give up their power in Afghanistan to the British. Great Britain and Russia now dominate Iran.

1906 Iran's first constitution and parliament is set up

1925 Reza Khan becomes Shah (Reza Shah Pahlavi)

1941 Reza Shah Pahlavi gives up the throne in favour of his son, Mohammed Reza Pahlavi

1951–1953 Iran nationalizes its oil industry

1962–1963 Ayatollah Khomeini is arrested and exiled

1979 The Shah is overthrown and leaves Iran. Ayatollah Khomeini returns to Iran to become leader of the Islamic Republic of Iran. Islamic militants take 52 Americans hostage at the US Embassy in Tehran.

1980–2005

1980 27 Jul.: The Shah dies of cancer in Egypt
22 Sept.: Iraq invades Iran. Eight years of war follow.

1981 20 Jan.: American hostages are freed after being held for 444 days

1988 3 Jul.: Iran Air aircraft carrying 290 passengers and crew is shot down over the Gulf by the US Navy
20 Jul.: Iran accepts ceasefire agreement with Iraq

1989 14 Feb.: Ayatollah Khomeini issues a fatwa against Salman Rushdie
3 Jun.: Ayatollah Khomeini dies
4 Jun.: President Khamene'i is appointed as the new leader

1995 The USA imposes oil and trade sanctions against Iran

1997 Mohammed Khatami wins the presidential election

1999 Pro-democracy students at Tehran University clash with the security forces

2000 Liberals and supporters of Khatami win 170 of the 290 seats in the Majlis elections

2001 President Khatami is re-elected for a second term
11 Sept.: Attacks on World Trade Center in New York City

2002 US President George Bush includes Iran in the 'Axis of Evil'
Sept.: Construction of Iran's first nuclear reactor continues

2003 Nov.: Iran suspends its uranium enrichment programme and allows tougher UN inspections of its nuclear facilities. An IAEA report concludes there is no evidence of a weapons programme.

2004 Feb.: Conservatives regain control of Iran's parliament
Nov.: Iran agrees once more to suspend its uranium enrichment plans

2005 Feb.: Iran announces it will form a common front with Syria against threats from the USA

51

Who's Who?

Ali and Hussein (the Shi'ite martyrs) Ali was born around 600 CE, and died in 661 CE. He was the son-in-law and cousin of the Prophet Mohammed, and was recognized as leader of the Muslim community by the Shi'ites in 656 CE. His rule was disputed by the Sunni 'Caliph' Mu'awiya, and he was murdered in 661 CE. He is buried in Najaf, Iraq. His son Hussein was born in 626 CE and was murdered by Sunni Muslims in 680 CE. He is buried in Karbala, Iraq.

Arafat, Yasser (Abu Ammar) Born in 1929 and died in 2004. Arafat claimed to have been born in Jerusalem, but spent much of his childhood and youth in Cairo, Egypt. Arafat studied civil engineering in Cairo and worked in Kuwait. He was a founding member of the anti-Israel guerrilla movement 'Fatah', in around 1959. Arafat was chairman of the Palestine Liberation Organization in 1969. He signed the Oslo peace accords with Israel in 1993. He became president of the Palestinian Authority in 1996.

Bazargan, Mehdi Born in 1907 and died in 1995. Bazargan trained as an engineer but entered politics in the early 1950s as Mossadegh's deputy prime minister. He was appointed by Ayatollah Khomeini as Iran's transitional prime minister in 1979.

Bin Laden, Osama Born in 1957, into a rich Saudi family. His father made a large fortune as a civil engineer, constructing buildings in Saudi Arabia and elsewhere in the Middle East. Bin Laden came under the influence of Islamic extremists while he was a student and went to Afghanistan to fight the occupying Soviet forces in 1979. He became a leader of the Islamic extremist faction opposed to all influence in the Middle East by the USA, and his organization, known as Al-Qaeda, approved, funded and helped to plan the 11 September attacks in the USA. Following the overthrow of the Taliban regime in Afghanistan in 2002, Osama bin Laden remained unfound.

Bush, George W. 43rd President of the USA (2001– due to leave office in 2009). Bush was born in 1946. He approved the invasion of Iraq in 2003. In 2005 he started to demand that Iran stop its nuclear programme.

Carter, James E. (Jimmy) 39th President of the USA (1977–1981). President Carter was born in 1924. He was US president during the hostage crisis in 1979–1981, when American diplomats were held in Tehran.

Cyrus the Great Born in 580 BCE and died in 529 BCE. King Cyrus created the Persian Empire by uniting the local peoples, and then went on to conquer Babylon and to subdue many other peoples. His lands stretched from the Mediterranean in the West as far as Peshawar in the East. King Cyrus was a ruler who won the trust of the people by establishing a system of law, which meant that each citizen could expect to be treated fairly by the state. He built a new capital for Persia in the province of Fars, and, according to Greek historians, invented the first true postal system.

Hussein, Saddam Born in 1937. Hussein is the former president of Iraq. He rose to power through the Iraqi Ba'ath Party. Hussein was captured by Coalition troops in December 2003.

Khamene'i, Ayatollah Born in the city of Mashhad in 1939. His father was a cleric, and he was raised in a religious atmosphere. At the age of 25, he achieved the highest honours in his religious studies at Qom. He rose within Iran's Shi'ite clergy and became close to Ayatollah Khomeini both as a friend and as a religious associate. From the moment of the Islamic Revolution, Ayatollah Khomeini placed him in increasingly responsible positions. In 1989 he was chosen by the Council of Guardians to succeed Ayatollah Khomeini as supreme leader.

Khatami, Mohammed Born in 1943. Khatami rose to the religious rank of hojjatoleslam (lower than that of ayatollah). He was part of Ayatollah Khomeini's circle, but had a different opinion on how the Islamic Republic should develop. He succeeded Ali Akbar Rafsanjani as president in 1997 when he won 70 per cent of the votes. Khatami is regarded as a reformist in Iran's political world. His plans as president were frustrated by losing the support of parliament. The Council of Guardians also halted some of the laws he wanted to pass.

Khomeini, Ayatollah Ruhollah Musavi, who later became Ayatollah Khomeini, was born in 1902 in the village of Khomein and died in 1989. He was educated as a cleric in the Shi'ite seminary in Qom, and took the name Khomeini. He became the senior figure in Shi'ite Islam in Iran, but because of his political activity, he was forced into exile by the Shah in 1964. Khomeini returned to Iran to found the Islamic Republic in 1979, and died after leading the country for ten years.

Kohl, Helmut Born in 1930. Kohl is a right-wing German politician. He was Chancellor of Germany (the highest political position, equivalent to prime minister) from 1982 until 1998. Kohl oversaw the reunification of Germany.

Mohammed The Prophet Mohammed was born in Mecca in 570 CE, and he died in Medina in 632 CE. He was brought up as a merchant by his uncle Abu Talib, and took up the successful business of trade across the desert to Syria, organizing caravans of camels to carry goods. In about 594 CE he married Khadijah, a wealthy widow. He was always a pious and philosophical man, and went on retreats to the desert where he meditated alone. From around 609 CE, he began to receive the text of the Qur'an from the Angel Gabriel who appeared to him in a cave where he was sleeping. He went on to found the Islamic faith and lead a growing community of Muslims in the Middle East.

Mossadegh, Mohammed Dr Mossadegh was born 1882 and died in 1967. He was prime minister of Iran from 1951 to 1953. He was a modern nationalist, who disapproved of Iran's monarchy. He nationalized Iran's oil industry in 1951, upsetting the West. In 1953 the Shah fled from Iran after trying unsuccessfully to force Mossadegh from office. However, Mossadegh was overthrown in a plot assisted by the CIA, the US intelligence service, and the Shah returned to Iran a few days later. The Shah put Mossadegh on trial for treason and held him under house arrest until his death.

Pahlavi, Mohammed Reza Shah The last Shah of Iran was born in 1919, and died in exile in 1980. The Shah was the ruler of Iran, and had succeeded his father to the throne in 1941. His father, Reza Shah, who had been an army general, was the first of the Pahlavi dynasty and was crowned as Shah in 1925. Mohammed Reza Shah became unpopular with his people, and when he attempted to bring in reforms, he was opposed by the Islamic clergy. He left Iran finally in 1979 as support for Khomeini grew stronger, and he died in Egypt in 1980.

Rafsanjani, Ali Akbar Hashemi Born in Rafsanjan, Iran, in 1934, where his father was a pistachio farmer. He rose to the religious rank of hojjatoleslam (lower than that of ayatollah). He was close to Ayatollah Khomeini from the start, and was speaker of Iran's parliament from 1980 to 1989. He won two elections and served as president of Iran for two terms from 1989 to 1997. He has been regarded as a conservative in internal politics, but also has links to the liberal former president Khatami. In 2000 he was elected to parliament for the first time. In the parliamentary elections of 2003, he led a new conservative alliance, which won a majority of the seats.

Reagan, Ronald 40th President of the USA (1981–1989). Reagan was born in 1911 and died in 2004. The US Embassy hostage crisis ended under Reagan.

Rushdie, Salman Born in 1947 in Mumbai (Bombay), India. Rushdie is a British writer. He is most famous for his book, *The Satanic Verses*, in which characters express views about Islam that some people believe are against the religion. Ayatollah Khomeini issued a fatwa against him in 1989. The fatwa condemned him to death by saying it was lawful for Muslims to kill him because of his blasphemy in the book. Rushdie has continued to write and publish novels and other works. However, he lived in hiding for some time and continues to be careful not to publicize his whereabouts.

Zoroaster A prophet in ancient Iran, who may have lived around 600 BCE. He founded a new religion in which a good god, Ahura Mazda, opposed an evil spirit, Ahriman. Human kind, he said, had been given the power to choose between good and evil. At the end of the world, good would triumph. This was the religion of Persia before the coming of Islam. The religion mainly survives today as the Parsi faith in India.

Find Out More

BOOKS FOR YOUNGER READERS

America Held Hostage: The Iran Hostage Crisis and the Iran-Contra Affair (Twentieth Century American History), Don Lawson and Barbara Feinberg (Franklin Watts, 1991)
Brings to life the hostage crisis and subsequent dealings between the USA and Iran's Islamic Republic.

Ayatollah Ruhollah Khomeini, Anne M Todd and Daniel E Harmon (Chelsea House Publishers, 2005)
A biography of Ayatollah Khomeini in a series on spiritual leaders and thinkers for younger readers.

Iran: A Primary Source Cultural Guide, Lauren Spencer (Rosen Publishing Group, 2004)
Well illustrated, this book looks at daily life, work and women's issues as well as history and politics.

BOOKS FOR OLDER READERS

Iran, Ali Ansari (Routledge Curzon, 2004)
Iranian author and specialist Ali Ansari sums up the most recent developments in Iran and the background of Iranian affairs.

The Iranian Labyrinth: Journeys through Theocratic Iran and its Furies, Dilip Hiro (Nation Books, 2005)
As Iran faces a showdown with the West over its nuclear ambitions, Middle East expert Dilip Hiro unravels the complexities of the Islamic Republic.

Persepolis: The Story of a Childhood, Marjane Satrapi (Jonathan Cape, 2003)
An Iranian teenager describes her life experiences in pictures and words.

The Persian Puzzle: The Conflict Between Iran and America, Kenneth Pollack (Random House, 2004)
Kenneth Pollack, a former CIA Iran analyst, looks at the political and cultural clash between Iran and the USA.

ADDRESSES TO WRITE TO

If you want to find out more about Iran and the Islamic Revolution, try contacting these organizations:

IN THE UK

The London Middle East Institute
Room 479
School of Oriental and African Studies
University of London
Russell Square
London WC1H OXG

The Royal Institute of International Affairs
Chatham House
10 St James's Square
London SW1Y 4LE

International Institute for Strategic Studies
Arundel House
13–15 Arundel Street
Temple Place
London WC2R 3DX

Council for Arab-British Understanding
1 Gough Square
London EC4A 3DE

IN AUSTRALIA

The Centre for Middle East and North African Studies
Macquarie University
Sydney 2109

The Centre for Middle Eastern and Central Asian Studies
Australian National University
Canberra ACT 0200

Index

Index

Titles in *The Middle East* series include:

Hardback   1-844-43206-8

Hardback   1-844-43205-X

Hardback   1-844-43204-1

Hardback   1-844-43203-3

Hardback   1-844-43207-6

Find out about other titles from Raintree on our website www.raintreepublishers.co.uk